Speak English for Success

ESL Conversations, Topics, and Dialogues

Reproducible

Lucia Gorea, Ph.D.

Dedicated to my son, Alex

AuthorHouse™
1663 Liberty Drive
Bloomington, IN 47403
www.authorhouse.com
Phone: 1-800-839-8640

First published by AuthorHouse 12/8/2009

ISBN: 978-1-4490-0207-7 (sc)

Library of Congress Control Number: 2009911865

Printed in the United States of America
Bloomington, Indiana

This book is printed on acid-free paper.

Cover design: Lucia Gorea

Editor: Karen Brattain

Cataloging Information*: Speak English for Success: ESL Conversations, Topics, and Dialogues*
Author: Lucia Gorea, Ph.D.
Language and Education

Table of Contents

Surprise Box

Divide the class into pairs or into groups of three or four. Have the students talk freely about the topics they draw from the box.

My First Love	My Last Job	My Favorite Season	Television	Horror Movies
Money	In the Jungle	Smoking	A Trip I Took	Earthquakes
My Home	Tattoos	Ghosts	My Parents	New Year's Celebration
Automobiles	Raising Children	Classical Music	Healthy Habits	The Qualities of a Good Employee
Friendship	Team Sports	My Favorite Games	A Day at the Beach	War and Peace

Topics for Discussion

Divide the class into small groups of three or four. Assign each student a different topic to discuss.

How will the world look four hundred years from now? Give details.	If you were given $1,000 to use for a good cause, what would you do? Explain.	What are the qualities of a good leader? Talk about a famous leader you admire.
If you were president of a poor country, what would your priorities be to help your country change? Name at least three.	You have to choose between rescuing a two-year-old boy or a mother of four from drowning. What is your choice? Explain.	Name four things you might see when you are dead. Use your imagination.
If you could go back in time, what year would you choose? Why?	What is your opinion about legalizing marijuana?	Name five things you might receive on New Year's Eve.
Does the violence on television affect the way people conduct themselves in real life? Comment on this subject.	Should students wear uniforms in school? State your opinion.	If you could change one thing about this world, what would it be? Explain.
Describe how disciplining children nowadays is different from the way you or your parents were disciplined in the past.	Should gay marriage be banned or legalized? State your opinion.	What should the government do about homeless people?
How can sexual and verbal abuse be prevented in both schools and families?	Describe the most dangerous experience you have ever had. Give details.	Are celebrities paid far more than they should be paid for movies or singing careers? State your opinion.

REPRODUCIBLE
Speak English for Success: ESL Conversations, Topics, and Dialogues

Lucia Gorea, Ph.D.

More Topics for Discussion

Divide the class into small groups of three or four. Assign each group a different topic to discuss.

How can we prevent global warming? What are the steps you suggest everyone should take to prevent this major problem?	The city council is considering building a prison in your neighborhood. How do you feel about having a prison near your home?
Is it a good idea for schools to use technology in classrooms? Does it affect learning in a positive or negative way? Explain.	Poverty has always been a major world concern. What can be done to eliminate poverty forever?
In your opinion, why do children drop out of school now more than ever? How can we prevent this from happening?	Many teenage girls become pregnant at a very early age. What can be done to solve this problem?
Do you believe in corporal punishment? Is spanking necessary in certain situations? Explain.	Can homelessness be prevented? What is your opinion?
Women work more than men but are paid less. Comment on this statement.	What should the government do to control violence and possession of guns in schools?
Do you agree or disagree with the following statement: Laws are too easy on sex offenders.	Do you believe that gays and lesbians should have the legal rights to get married and adopt children? State your opinion.

Newspaper Headlines

Pair up with a partner and create stories based on the headlines below.

TOP STORIES

Secret Santa Who Gave Away $1.3 Million Dies

New York City Subway Hero Saves Woman

Tsunami Warning in Japan

A Death in Acapulco

Is Marriage No Longer a Must?

Two Dead in Small Jet Crash

Adoption Controversy

How to Pay Off Holiday Debt

Missing Boy Found Alive after Two Years

Bilingualism Delays Onset of Dementia

Women Accused of Negligent Homicide in Wreck That Killed Teen

Man Files Lawsuit to Take Wife's Name

Death of Shark Leaves Scientists Grasping

Money Doesn't Talk

Family Dramas Continue after Celebrity Deaths

Glitz, Hits, and Splits

Get Started

Cut along the lines. Divide students into groups of three or four and give each group an envelope that contains these topics. Students take turns talking for three minutes about each topic they draw from the envelope.

My Hobbies
My High School Years
An Animal I Would Like to Be
My Hometown
How I Cook My Favorite Food
My First Date
My Career Goals
My Favorite Book
Shopping
Photography
Camping
Volunteering
Healthy Marriage Tips
Yawning
Recycling
Crime
My Birthday Celebration
My Favorite Place
My Daily Routine
Cheating

Let's Talk!

Interview your partner. Share your answers with your group or with the whole class.

Talk about something you have never done.
Talk about something you would never do.
Talk about something you love to do.
Talk about something you hate to do.
Talk about something you would like to give others.
Talk about something you could never eat.
Talk about something you would lie about.
Talk about something you would never forget.
Talk about something you should not leave unattended.
Talk about something you might lose at a party.
Talk about something you should never complain about.
Talk about something you should be proud of.

REPRODUCIBLE
Speak English for Success: ESL Conversations, Topics, and Dialogues

Lucia Gorea, Ph.D.

Let's Talk More!

Interview your partner. Share your answers with your group or with the whole class.

Talk about a movie you saw recently.
Talk about a concert you attended.
Talk about a book you enjoyed reading.
Talk about a teacher you admired in school.
Talk about a place you often visit.
Talk about a future invention.
Talk about your vacation plans.
Talk about a childhood friend.
Talk about your favorite actor or actress.
Talk about your dream house.
Talk about your favorite subject in school.
Talk about the weather in your country.

Tell Me about Yourself

- What is your name? How do you spell it?
- Where are you from? Describe your hometown.
- How long have you been in this country? How long do you plan to stay here? Where do you live?
- What is the purpose of your visit to this country?
- How many members of your family came with you to this country?
- How big is your family? Is family important to you?
- What are your mother's best qualities?
- What are your father's best qualities?
- Whom do you resemble the most?
- How would you describe a perfect family?
- Do you work? If so, what kind of work do you do?
- What is your educational background?
- What is your marital status? Do you have any children?
- What are your hobbies?
- Tell me about your childhood. What is your best childhood memory?
- What is your worst childhood memory?
- What are your personal goals? What are your career goals?
- What are your good habits? What are your bad habits?
- Describe yourself with five adjectives.
- Tell me something special about yourself.
- Is there anything you would like to change about yourself?

Your turn: Ask your partner three questions about the same topic.

1. _____
2. _____
3. _____

Friends

- Do you have any friends? How many do you have?
- How would you define friendship? What are the qualities of a good friend?
- What does the following saying mean: "A real friend is one who walks in when the rest of the world walks out."
- How often do you see your friends?
- Do you have any long-distance friendships? Do you chat with these friends online, or do you prefer sending letters?
- Describe your best friend. Do you share the same ideals, the same interests, or the same opinions?
- What are the best places to meet friends? Do you make friends easily?
- Are you "friends" with your parents? Do you believe that maintaining a close relationship with your family helps you become a better person in life?
- Whom do you share your secrets with? Do you trust your friends? Are your secrets safe with them?
- Can people live without friends?
- Do you have the following saying in your language: "Birds of a feather flock together." Explain what the saying means.
- What do you usually do when you get together with friends?
- Have your friends ever let you down? How did you react?
- Can your best friend become your lover? Explain.
- Can a lover become your best friend? Explain.
- What would you do if your friend "stole" your girlfriend or boyfriend?
- How would you react if your lifelong friend cheated on you with your partner?
- Do you consider yourself a good friend? Are there any areas you would like to improve in your relationships with others?
- Do you believe that a difference in age can become an obstacle to friendship? Are your friends the same age as you?
- What advice would you give to people who do not need friends in their lives?

Your turn: Ask your partner three questions about the same topic.

1.

2.

3.

Cultural Issues: Similarities and Differences

- What is culture shock?
- Have you ever experienced culture shock when you arrived in a new country?
- Are you homesick?
- Have you made friends in your new country? Who are they?
- How do you socialize? Do you believe that meeting people through communities, schools, or churches is a good way to adjust to a new culture?
- What do you miss most about your hometown?
- What do you like about your culture? Is there anything you would like to change about it?
- What are the main points of interest in your country?
- Whom do you admire most in your culture? Is there anyone you admire in your new culture?
- Are there many differences between your native culture and your new one? Name a few.
- How do people celebrate New Year's Day in your country? Is this an important holiday to celebrate?
- In your country, how many meals a day do people have, and which one is considered the most important one? What do you usually eat for breakfast, lunch, and dinner?
- Tell me about the way you celebrate weddings in your country.
- What are your religious beliefs?
- Would it be a problem if someone married a person of a different religion or culture?
- How do people spend their leisure time in your country?
- Describe the way students and teachers interact with each other.
- What is the relationship between parents and children in your country? Do they get along well? Are parents strict? How do they discipline their children?
- How do people greet each other in your culture?
- How do you celebrate your birthday? Do you receive any presents?
- Name five similarities between your culture and the one you live in now.

Your turn: Ask your partner three questions about the same topic.

1. _____
2. _____
3. _____

Learning Languages

- What is your native language?
- How many letters or characters are there in your alphabet?
- Do you know how many letters there are in the English alphabet?
- How many dialects do people speak in your country?
- How many languages do you speak?
- Are the sounds in your language difficult to pronounce? Give me some examples.
- How do you say, "Hello, how are you?" in your language?
- How do you introduce yourself in your country?
- Is writing in your language more difficult than speaking? How about in English?
- What is the most difficult for you in the process of learning English: speaking, listening, reading, writing, grammar, or pronunciation? Please explain.
- What are the most difficult sounds for you to pronounce in English?
- What are some good ways to learn English? Do you watch movies? Do you read newspapers or magazines? Do you borrow books from your local library or socialize in a community center?
- Do you believe that copying words from dictionaries or textbooks helps you improve your writing skills? Explain.
- In order to improve your English, do you prefer listening to recordings or talking with native speakers? Explain.
- Do you speak English with your friends or family? Why? Why not?
- How many hours do you study every day? How many words do you learn on a daily basis? Do you do your homework regularly?
- What is the easiest way for you to learn a new language?
- Are you a fast learner?
- There are three types of learners: visual, aural, and kinesthetic. Which type of learner are you?
- What are the qualities of a good student? What are the qualities of a good teacher?
- If you were an English teacher for a day, how would you teach your class? Explain.
- Did you study English in your native country? If so, for how long?
- Is English the foreign language most spoken in your country?
- What is the main reason you study English?

Your turn: Ask your partner three questions about the same topic.

1. _____

2. _____

3. _____

Education

- Is education important? Why? Why not?
- Is homework necessary to help students reinforce what they have learned in class?
- Should students be assigned daily homework? State your opinion.
- Would you prefer going to school every day or having home schooling? Explain.
- Nowadays people are busier than ever, raising families and building careers. Would you consider online education in order to obtain your graduate degree? Explain.
- In your opinion, who are the best educators, teachers or parents?
- Do you believe that students should study by themselves or with the help of their parents?
- Are grades important? Do they always reflect your knowledge?
- What is or was your favorite subject in school?
- Who is or was your favorite teacher?
- In many countries of the world children don't have access to education. How can we help solve this important problem?
- Uniforms are no longer required in most schools. Do you think uniforms should be mandatory? Why? Why not?
- Do you think that teenagers nowadays have lost respect for teachers and parents? Do they have liberties and privileges that long ago were considered offensive?
- How is school today different from the school your parents or grandparents attended? Which one do you prefer?
- Describe a day in your life as a student.
- If you could introduce one new subject in the school curriculum, what would it be, and why?
- Is there anything you would like to change in today's educational system?
- If you were the Secretary of Education in your country, what major changes would you make, and what school regulations would you implement?
- Describe the ideal school. Describe the ideal student. Describe the ideal teacher.
- What are your fondest memories of school?
- A Chinese proverb says, "Teachers open the door, but you must enter by yourself." Do you agree? Comment on the proverb.

Your turn: Ask your partner three questions about the same topic.

1. _____

2. _____

3. _____

REPRODUCIBLE
Speak English for Success: ESL Conversations, Topics, and Dialogues
Lucia Gorea, Ph.D.

Dating and Relationships

- Do you believe in love at first sight? Why or why not?
- Do you fall in love easily? Have you ever had a crush on someone (your neighbor, your classmate, your boss)?
- What are the qualities you seek in a partner?
- Have you ever been on a blind date? If so, was it a good experience?
- Have you ever been "head over heels in love" with someone? Are you still in that same relationship?
- Have you dated someone much older or much younger than you? Do you believe that age is a serious factor in dating someone and in keeping that relationship stable?
- Should age be something that comes in the way of a person's marriage?
- How many girlfriends or boyfriends have you dumped?
- What do you do after a breakup?
- Have you found Mr. Right or Miss Right yet?
- Do you respect your partner? Do you believe in mutual respect?
- Who should pay the restaurant bill, you or your partner?
- Do you believe in arranged marriages?
- Should a couple stay engaged for a period of time before marriage? Why? Why not?
- What is more important, love or wealth? Can a lack of wealth ruin marriage?
- What are the qualities of a good wife? What are the qualities of a good husband?
- Do you think people change after getting married?
- Do you think getting married means giving up freedom?
- Should people stay married if they do not get along and if they argue every day? What if they have children?
- Should women tolerate verbal and physical abuse for the sake of their children?
- Why do so many people stay single? What are the reasons they do not get married?
- What do you think of same-sex marriage?
- How would you describe a perfect marriage?
- If you are married, describe your wedding day. If you are single, describe your dream wedding.
- Comment on the following statement: "Marriage is a mirror in which one sees a reflection of oneself."

Your turn: Ask your partner three questions about the same topic.

1. _____
2. _____
3. _____

Jobs and Employment

- Do you have a job now? Where do you work? What is your present occupation?
- Are you a blue-collar worker or a white-collar worker?
- What was your job in your country? Did you like it? Did you make a good living?
- Which days of the week do you work?
- Do you work full time or part time? Describe your work schedule.
- How many hours of overtime do you work? What is the pay for overtime?
- What is your educational background? Do you plan to pursue a career in your new country?
- What is your work experience? What jobs or work experience have you had before?
- Do you like to work with other people or alone?
- What are your work skills?
- Does your supervisor or manager help you when you have a problem?
- Have you ever been injured at work? How did you deal with this situation?
- Have you ever been fired? If so, explain.
- Have you ever quit your job? If so, what was the reason?
- What are the qualities of a good employer? What are the qualities of a good employee?
- What are your career goals?
- In what ways are the jobs in your new country similar to or different from the jobs in your native country?
- Where would you like to work five years from now? What can you do to prepare for that job?
- What salary would you like to earn in the future?
- Do you work in a safe environment? Do you wear safety gear?
- Name three reasons why you might be fired from a job. Name three behaviors that will help you keep your job.

Your turn: Ask your partner three questions about the same topic.

1. _____
2. _____
3. _____

Healthy Habits

- Are you currently dieting?
- Have you ever been on a diet? If so, for how long? What did your diet consist of?
- Do you believe that eating three meals a day is important? Why? Why not?
- How many meals a day do you eat?
- Do you snack? If so, what do you snack on?
- Do you prefer soda pop to fruit juice?
- Do vitamins play an important role in keeping us healthy? Explain.
- How many servings of fruits and vegetables do you eat a day?
- Do you ever count calories?
- Do you read labels on packages before you purchase food items?
- Do you read the expiration date on canned and frozen foods?
- Do you exercise regularly? If so, what type of exercise do you do?
- Does your family join you in your daily workout? Why? Why not?
- Nowadays, both children and adults have the tendency to become overweight. How do you prevent obesity?
- Do you believe that obesity is the main cause of many diseases? Explain.
- Do you eat fast food? If so, how often? What is your favorite fast food?
- What is the Food Guide Pyramid? Do you follow its guidelines?
- How many hours a night do you sleep? How can you prevent insomnia?
- Do you smoke? Does someone in your family smoke?
- What are some major concerns that smoking raises today?
- Would you convince someone dear to you to quit smoking? What would your arguments be?
- How do you stay healthy?

Your turn: Ask your partner three questions about the same topic.

1. _____
2. _____
3. _____

Food

- Do you like to eat? What is your favorite food?
- How often do you eat out?
- Where do you eat when you go out? Do you prefer fancy restaurants or fast-food restaurants?
- Do you like to cook? Why or why not?
- Do you drink coffee every morning? How many cups of coffee do you drink each day?
- What is your favorite drink?
- Do you drink water? If so, how many glasses a day?
- How many meals do you have a day? Do you skip meals?
- What do you usually have for breakfast?
- What do you usually have for lunch?
- What do you usually have for dinner?
- Do you eat snacks? If so, what do you eat?
- How often do you eat junk food?
- Do you eat fruits and vegetables daily?
- Are you a vegetarian?
- How often do you eat meat?
- Have you ever been on a diet? If so, for how long?
- Do you like sweets? Do you prefer chocolate, candy, or ice cream?
- How often do you eat dessert after dinner?
- Do you read the nutritional information on the foods you buy?
- Have you ever eaten food from other countries? Chinese, Japanese, Thai, African, Polish, American, French, Italian?
- Have you ever eaten snake soup? frog legs, camel meat, dog meat, pork liver, monkey brains, horse meat, quail meat, squid, snails, sheep, rabbit?

Your turn: Ask your partner three questions about the same topic.

1. _____
2. _____
3. _____

REPRODUCIBLE
Speak English for Success: ESL Conversations, Topics, and Dialogues
Lucia Gorea, Ph.D.

Holidays

- What is your favorite holiday?
- Do you celebrate it with your family?
- Do you go to church or temple on that day? Are there any specific prayers or blessings that go with that day?
- Is gift giving a part of this holiday?
- What is the best present you have ever received?
- How do you prepare for this holiday? Do you cook specific foods on that day?
- What is your favorite holiday food? What is your favorite holiday song?
- Do you decorate your house on this holiday? Describe how you decorate.
- Are cards sent or given for this holiday?
- Do you buy new clothes on that day?
- Do people sing songs or carols on holidays?
- Do you visit your family on holidays?
- What games do you play during holidays?
- Do you read stories to the little ones in the house?
- What kind of music do you listen to during this time?
- Have you ever been to any holiday concerts? Which one did you enjoy the most?
- What are some of your fondest memories of Christmas or New Year's Day?
- Do you celebrate Easter? If so, what do you do on that holiday?
- How many holidays do you celebrate each year?
- Do you celebrate religious holidays?
- What are some of the national and religious holidays that people celebrate in your country? Are there any rituals performed on these special days?
- Do you like traveling, or you prefer staying home on holidays?
- Do you have a funny memory you would like to share with others?
- Do you think holidays are important?
- What are your plans for next year's holidays?

Your turn: Ask your partner three questions about the same topic.

1. _____
2. _____
3. _____

Traveling

- Have you ever been abroad?
- How many countries have you visited so far?
- What is the most memorable place you have ever been to? Would you visit that place again? Why? Why not?
- What is the scariest trip you have ever taken?
- Do you like to travel alone or accompanied by family or friends?
- Do you prefer to travel by bus, by plane, by car, or by train?
- Have you ever missed a plane or a train? What did you do?
- Have you ever been on a cruise? If so, what did you see? Would you recommend that cruise to someone else?
- Do you book your tickets online or at a travel agency? Which one is more efficient? Is it safe to book online?
- How many pieces of luggage do you take with you on a trip?
- What do you pack for a two-week trip abroad? Name five items you always take with you on a trip.
- Where do you keep your documents and money or traveler's checks?
- Have you ever been mugged? If so, how did you react?
- Have you ever hitchhiked? Is it safe to hitchhike in your country?
- Do you buy souvenirs in countries you visit? If so, what do you usually buy?
- What places would you like to visit? What is your dream vacation?
- Do you prefer summer vacations or winter vacations? Talk about some activities you can do in these seasons.
- What do you like to visit in a foreign country? Do you usually carry a map and a tourist guide with you? Are you an adventurer?
- Describe a day in your life when you are in a foreign place.
- Describe your best trip.
- Describe your worst trip.

Your turn: Ask your partner three questions about the same topic.

1. _____
2. _____
3. _____

Sports

- Do you like sports? What is your favorite sport?
- Are you good at sports? What did you play in high school?
- Do you like summer sports or winter sports? Name a few.
- Do you ski or snowboard? Do you play tennis? Do you play basketball?
- Can you ride a bike? How old were you when you first rode a bike?
- Do you like to exercise? If so, how often do you exercise?
- Is exercise important to your health?
- Do you prefer working out or watching television?
- Is jogging an important physical activity in your country?
- What is the most popular sport in your country?
- What do you prefer, watching games on television or going to the stadium? Do you watch games alone or with friends?
- Can you name some dangerous sports? Do you play any?
- Do you like hiking?
- Have you ever gone rafting?
- Have you ever gone parachuting or gliding?
- Have you ever been horseback riding?
- Are you a good swimmer?
- How did you learn to swim?
- Would you rather go skiing or surfing?
- Have you ever been injured while you were playing a sport?
- Have you ever participated in a sports competition?
- Have you ever won a medal in a game?
- Which Olympic sports do you like to watch on TV?
- Who is your favorite athlete or player? Have you ever met a sports celebrity? If not, whom would you like to meet in the future?

Your turn: Ask your partner three questions about the same topic.

1. _____
2. _____
3. _____

Shopping and Fashion

- Do you like going shopping?
- Do you usually shop by yourself or with a friend or relative?
- Where do you usually shop, at small boutiques or in large department stores? Explain.
- Do you buy secondhand clothes?
- Do you spend a lot of money on clothing? If so, how much do you spend in a month?
- What do you buy more often, shoes or clothes? Explain.
- How often do you buy accessories? What kind of accessories do you buy?
- Do you wear makeup? Do you like women who wear makeup, or you prefer a more natural look?
- What is your opinion about tattoos? Is this something you would consider for yourself or your children? Do tattoos affect the way people think of you?
- Do you have facial or body piercings? Does piercing change your image in society?
- Do you like wearing high heels? What do you think of women who wear high heels? Is this appropriate in your country?
- Do men wear their hair long or short in your country? Which look do you prefer?
- Do you wear gloves or hats? If you do, on what occasions?
- How do your parents and grandparents dress differently than you?
- What do you like to wear most—traditional, more sophisticated clothes or more casual sports outfits?
- What would you wear to a job interview?
- What do you wear at work or at school? How about at a party?
- Would you ever consider modeling for a fashion show? What is your opinion about the modeling industry?
- Do you buy fashion magazines? If so, which ones?
- Have you ever been to a fashion show? Do you watch fashion shows on television? Does the clothing they present inspire you?
- Do you agree that the clothes you wear reflect who you are inside?
- Are you wearing the same size clothes this year as you wore five years ago?
- Describe your best outfit.

Your turn: Ask your partner three questions about the same topic.

1. _____
2. _____
3. _____

Pets

- Do you have pets? What kind of pets do you have?
- Do you consider yourself a pet lover?
- Do you prefer cats or dogs?
- How do you take care of your pet? Do you bathe and brush your pet?
- When you are away, who takes care of your pet?
- Do you clean up after your pet all the time?
- Do you talk to your pet? If so, what do you say?
- How often do you walk your pet?
- Do you know someone who keeps reptiles or pigs in the house as pets?
- What are the most common animals people have as pets in your country?
- Are you afraid of spiders?
- What are you most frightened of?
- How do people in your country take care of their pets?
- Is it appropriate for a dog or a cat to sleep in the same bed with its owner?
- Does your pet know any tricks?
- Do you believe that aggressive dogs should be muzzled? Why? Why not?
- Have you taken your pet to an obedience class or training? Did it help?
- What should pet owners do if their dogs or cats make a mess or chew furniture?
- Do you believe that animals need affection?
- Do you give your pet treats?
- How do you discipline your pet?
- How many pets should people keep in their homes?
- Comment on the following Latin proverb: "Beware of a silent dog and still water."

Your turn: Ask your partner three questions about the same topic.

1. _____
2. _____
3. _____

Music

- Do you like music?
- What kind of music do you like?
- Do you prefer classical music or pop?
- Who is your favorite composer?
- Who is your favorite singer?
- What is your favorite band?
- Can you play a musical instrument? If so, when did you start playing it?
- Can someone in your family play a musical instrument?
- Can you name a few famous composers? Who is the most popular composer in your culture?
- Did you study music in school? When was the last time you went to a concert?
- Whom do you prefer, John Lennon or ACDC?
- Have you ever listened to punk music?
- Do you enjoy country music? Who is your favorite country singer?
- Do you like watching music videos? Can you name your favorite music video?
- Do you listen to music while driving? working? exercising?
- What was the last CD you bought?
- Do you like being alone when you listen to music?
- Has your musical taste changed over the years?
- How does music make you feel?
- How does music affect people?
- Does music have the power to heal sick people?
- Would the world be the same without music?

Your turn: Ask your partner three questions about the same topic.

1. _____
2. _____
3. _____

Movies and Entertainment

- How often do you watch movies?
- Do you prefer watching movies alone or with friends?
- Do you like renting movies or going to the movie theater?
- Do you like horror movies? Why? Why not? Explain.
- Do you prefer romantic movies or comedies?
- Talk about your favorite movie of all time. Who was in it? Who was the director?
- What is the worst movie you have ever seen? What aspects of the movie did you not like?
- What is the funniest movie you have ever seen? Who is your favorite comedian?
- Do you like visiting museums? What was the last one you visited?
- Have you ever been to a castle? How did you like the visit?
- Would you prefer going to an amusement park or camping?
- What are some of the most popular amusement parks in your country?
- How often do you go to a concert? What was the last concert you went to? Do you usually go alone or with friends?
- Would you rather go to a rock concert or to a Broadway musical?
- Have you ever been on stage and performed in front of an audience? If so, please describe your experience. Did you have stage fright?
- Have you ever been on TV? If so, what show was it?
- Do you consider going to literary events? Do you like poetry or short stories? Are you a writer?
- Do you read books? What is your favorite book? Is there an author whose books you enjoy a lot?
- Are you a gambler? What happens when your luck runs out?
- What is your opinion about people who gamble?
- Do you have a casino in your hometown?
- Name five forms of entertainment you enjoy in your spare time.

Your turn: Ask your partner three questions about the same topic.

1. _____
2. _____
3. _____

Crime

- What kinds of crime are most common in your country?
- Are there any places in your city where the crime rate is high?
- Is it safe to walk by yourself after dark in your city?
- Have you ever been robbed? How did you react?
- Have you ever witnessed a crime? What did you do?
- What would you do if you saw that a person was being mugged?
- Have you ever stolen anything?
- How is crime punished in your country?
- What do you think of capital punishment? Explain.
- Do you believe in corporal punishment?
- What is the punishment for murder in your country? Should murderers be executed, or should they be sentenced to life in prison?
- What is the punishment for stealing in your country? Should thieves go to jail for stealing? State your opinion.
- What is the punishment for sexual abuse or rape in your country?
- Are laws too easy or too harsh on criminals?
- If you had the power to change the laws in your country, what would your priority be?
- What would you do if you heard a burglar in your house?
- What would you do if you saw two strangers on your property?
- Is your house provided with an alarm system? Is it important to have such a device?
- Do you or does someone in your house carry a weapon? Is the possession of weapons legal in your country? Is it safe to keep weapons in your house when you have children? Where should people keep their weapons in order to avoid accidents?
- How can you prevent crime?
- Do you have emergency phone numbers handy in case you need to call and report a crime?
- Do you think that crime prevention should be discussed and taught more in schools or homes?
- Have you ever been the victim of a crime?

Your turn: Ask your partner three questions about the same topic.

1. _____
2. _____
3. _____

In Case of Emergency

- Have you ever been in a disaster? What are the common disasters in your country?
- Are you prepared for a disaster?
- Do you have a special plan for all family members?
- Have you packed an emergency kit? What are the basics you need to survive? Do you have enough bottled water and canned foods stored to last you at least a week?
- What are some basic items you would pack for babies, children, adults, seniors, and people with disabilities? What about for your pets? Make a list.
- Do you have an emergency car kit? What does it contain?
- Have you attended any emergency preparedness classes or workshops?
- If so, what have you learned?
- Have you participated in any fire or earthquake drills?
- Are there any natural disasters that might occur in your area?
- What are they?
- Do you have a fire extinguisher in your house? Have you ever used it?
- Is your house equipped with smoke detectors? How many do you have in your house?
- Have you installed a security alert system in your house? How can you prevent your house from being broken into?
- Where do you keep a flashlight? What do you do in case of a power outage?
- Is there a telephone next to your bed? Do you keep a list with emergency phone numbers handy?
- Have you ever been in a dangerous situation? What did you do?
- How should people prepare for disasters? What is your advice?

Your turn: Ask your partner three questions about the same topic.

1. _____
2. _____
3. _____

Major World Issues

- Do you believe that global warming is going to affect our generation at all? How about the generations to come?
- What is the greenhouse effect? Does it affect our climate?
- What are some of the causes of global warming?
- Is the sea level rising? If so, can it have a negative impact on our globe?
- What can we do to slow down the global warming process?
- In many countries of the world, women are oppressed, abused by their husbands or other family members, and enslaved. What could and should we do to eliminate violence toward women?
- Religion has always played an important role in family structure and in the way many people think and act. Is it positive or negative that religion plays such an important role in our lives?
- AIDS/HIV causes thousands of deaths every year in many parts of the world. Can this deadly disease be prevented? Explain.
- What advice do you give to teenagers to help them avoid being infected with HIV?
- In Africa, people die from hunger every day. Infants and children die from starvation, while in other parts of the world a lot of food is thrown in the garbage every day. Is there a way to balance this situation?
- Teenagers find drinking and smoking very entertaining. They slowly become addicted to these vices that affect their health and sometimes cost them their lives. What is your advice to their parents? Can schools do something about this problem?
- Drugs affect people's thinking and destroy their lives. If it was in your power, what would you do to solve this problem?
- Amnesty International is a worldwide movement of people who campaign for internationally recognized human rights for all. Would you like to join this organization? If so, how could you contribute?
- What does UNICEF stand for?
- What can you do to protect children from violence, exploitation, and abuse?

Your turn: Ask your partner three questions about the same topic.

1. _____

2. _____

3. _____

Miscellaneous Questions

- Have you ever ridden a camel?
- Can you knit socks?
- Are you right-handed or left-handed? Are you ambidextrous?
- Do you sing in the shower? What is your favorite tune?
- Have you ever slept for twenty-four hours?
- Do you sleep on the right side of the bed?
- Have you ever won something?
- How many times have you been in love?
- What is your greatest fear?
- What color are your socks?
- Have you ever lost something valuable?
- What's under your bed?
- Would you like to go bungee jumping?
- Have you ever fallen asleep while bathing?
- Describe a very embarrassing moment.
- Are you afraid of ghosts? Have you ever seen one?
- Have you cheated on a test?
- Have you ever lied to your parents? If so, what was it about?
- Are you superstitious?
- Have you ever slept in a cave?
- Have you ever gotten lost in the woods?
- What would you do if you had $1 million?

Your turn: Ask your partner three questions about the same topic.

1. _____
2. _____
3. _____

Who Am I? Famous People

Am I a man? Am I alive? Am I a singer? Answers: Yes or No

Cut into slips of paper and pin a celebrity's name on each student's back. Each student will circulate and ask about the celebrity's name. Only yes or no questions are allowed. Play until everyone has guessed who he or she is.

Mother Teresa	Brad Pitt	Michael Jackson
George W. Bush	Shaquille O'Neal	Queen Elizabeth
Madonna	Einstein	Harry Potter
Beethoven	Bill Gates	John Lennon
Napoléon	Oprah	Shakespeare
Nelson Mandela	Britney Spears	Picasso

What Am I? Animals

Am I big? Am I a swimmer? Do I hop? Answers: Yes or No

Cut into slips of paper and pin an animal's name on each student's back. Each student will circulate and ask about the animal's name. Only yes or no questions are allowed. Play until everyone has guessed who he or she is.

monkey	elephant	kangaroo
crocodile	whale	tiger
horse	rabbit	penguin
leopard	mouse	snake
cow	pig	camel
zebra	polar bear	eagle

What Am I? Fruits

Am I red? Am I sweet? Am I seedless? Answers: Yes or No

Cut into slips of paper and pin the name of a fruit on each student's back. Each student will circulate and ask about the fruit's name. Only yes or no questions are allowed. Play until everyone has guessed who he or she is.

orange	banana	watermelon
kiwi	strawberry	peach
papaya	apple	avocado
pineapple	cherry	apricot
plum	lemon	grapefruit
mango	pear	nectarine

What Am I? Vegetables

Am I round? Am I green? Am I leafy? Answers: Yes or No

Cut into slips of paper and pin the name of a vegetable on each student's back. Each student will circulate and ask about the vegetable's name. Only yes or no questions are allowed. Play until everyone has guessed who he or she is.

cabbage	spinach	potato
pepper	cucumber	onion
pumpkin	lettuce	tomato
eggplant	mushroom	celery
broccoli	cauliflower	corn
turnip	garlic	carrot

Famous Sayings

Pair up with a partner and comment on the following sayings. Give examples from real-life situations.

Aristotle:
"Education is the best provision for the journey to old age."

John F. Kennedy:
"Ask not what your country can do for you—ask what you can do for your country."

Mark Twain:
"Always do right. This will gratify some people and astonish the rest."

Aesop:
"We would often be sorry if our wishes were granted."

Albert Einstein:
"The world is a dangerous place to live; not because of the people who are evil, but because of the people who don't do anything about it."

Mahatma Gandhi:
"You must not lose faith in humanity. Humanity is an ocean; if a few drops of the ocean are dirty, the ocean does not become dirty."

Abraham Cowley:
"Of all ills that one endures, hope is a cheap and universal cure."

Abraham Lincoln:
"Better to remain silent and be thought a fool than to speak out and remove all doubt."

Oscar Wilde:
"It is better to be beautiful than to be good, but it is better to be good than to be ugly."

Voltaire:
"I may disagree with what you have to say, but I shall defend, to the death, your right to say it."

Maya Angelou:
"It is this belief in a power larger than myself and other than myself which allows me to venture into the unknown and even the unknowable."

Plato:
"Be kind, for everyone you meet is fighting a harder battle."

Speak English for Success: ESL Conversations, Topics, and Dialogues
Lucia Gorea, Ph.D.

Martin Luther King, Jr.:
"We are prone to judge success by the index of our salaries or the size of our automobile rather than by the quality of our service and relationship to mankind."

Mother Teresa:
"Being unwanted, unloved, uncared for, forgotten by everybody, I think that is a much greater hunger, a much greater poverty than the person who has nothing to eat."

Socrates:
"Bad men live that they may eat and drink, whereas good men eat and drink that they may live."

Confucius:
"It does not matter how slow you go as long as you do not stop."

Thomas A. Edison:
"Many of life's failures are people who did not realize how close they were to success when they gave up."

George Bernard Shaw:
"A life spent making mistakes is not only more honorable, but more useful than a life spent doing nothing."

Sophocles:
"Truly, to tell lies is not honorable; but when the truth entails tremendous ruin, to speak dishonorably is pardonable."

Samuel Johnson:
"Nothing has more retarded the advancement of learning than the disposition of vulgar minds to ridicule and vilify what they do not understand."

Thomas Edison:
"What man's mind can create, man's character can control."

Ralph Waldo Emerson:
"What lies behind us and what lies ahead of us are tiny matters compared to what lives within us."

"If" Sentences

If you could be any person, who would you choose to be?	If you inherited an enormous fortune, how would you spend it?
If you could be any animal, what would you be?	If your best friend committed an awful crime, how would you react?
If you lost your passport in a foreign country and had to return back home the next day, what would you do?	If you were fired from a job for a wrong reason, what would you do or say?
If you saw a hit-and-run accident, how would you react?	If you could change one thing about yourself, what would it be?
If you could go back in time, what year would you choose to go to?	If you were the leader of your country, what changes would you bring?
If you had supernatural powers, what would you do?	If a classmate cheated on a test, what would you do or say?

More "If" Sentences

If you were the only survivor in a plane crash, how would you react?	If you were boating and suddenly large waves and winds pulled your boat far from the shore, what would you do?
If you noticed that one of your friends was doing drugs, what would you say to him or her?	If you were alone in the house at night and heard someone walking toward your bedroom, what would you do?
If you were given the possibility of dining with a celebrity, whom would you choose?	If you found a wallet on the street with an ID card and $200, what would you do?
If your boss were rude to you, what would you say to him or her?	If you had dinner at your boss's house and you didn't like the food at all, what would you say or do?
If a member of your family filed for divorce, what would you do to help?	If you were stuck in traffic and you had a plane to catch in forty-five minutes, what would you do?
If a classmate or coworker asked you for a large amount of money to pay his rent, what would you say or do?	If you were trapped in a snowstorm with no means of communication, how would you survive?

Up Close and Personal

Individually, make questions and answer them. Then work in pairs, and compare your answers to those of your partner.

- name:
    Q: _____
    A: _____

- country of origin:
    Q: _____
    A: _____

- native language:
    Q: _____
    A: _____

- large or small family:
    Q: _____
    A: _____

- teacher:
    Q: _____
    A: _____

- previous work:
    Q: _____
    A: _____

- volunteer:
    Q: _____
    A: _____

- lunch:
    Q: _____
    A: _____

- wake up:
    Q: _____
    A: _____

- go to bed:
  - Q: _____
  - A: _____

- hobbies:
  - Q: _____
  - A: _____

- career goals:
  - Q: _____
  - A: _____

- next vacation:
  - Q: _____
  - A: _____

- driving test:
  - Q: _____
  - A: _____

- amazing experience:
  - Q: _____
  - A: _____

- embarrassing situation:
  - Q: _____
  - A: _____

- recent museum:
  - Q: _____
  - A: _____

- in the summer:
  - Q: _____
  - A: _____

- a memorable day:
  - Q: _____
  - A: _____

- strengths:
  - Q: _____
  - A: _____

What Would You Say Or Do?

What are the possible consequences of the situations below? How would you solve each situation? Share your ideas in small groups.

1.

You are at work, and you have to call the landlord regarding your house payment, which is due tomorrow. You need to explain that you will be one week late. You know that the management is very strict and that your company's policy does not allow phone calls except for one-minute emergency ones. What do you do?	
Possible consequences	Solutions
Share your answers with a partner. In pairs, create a dialogue.	

2.

This is the third time you are late for work. You are very worried. You leave the house early each time, but traffic or accidents on the road prevent you from arriving on time. The boss is waiting for you with an angry face. What do you say?	
Possible consequences	Solutions
Share your answers with a partner. In pairs, create a dialogue.	

3.

You are on the bus touring a city in Canada, and suddenly you get off in a hurry when the bus comes to a stop. You just saw the museum you wanted to visit. Then you realize that you forgot your purse with your ID, credit cards and money on the bus. What do you do?	
Possible Consequences	Solutions
Share your answers with a partner. In pairs, create a dialogue.	

4.

The waiter serves you breakfast and accidentally drops the whole cup of coffee on your table and on your suit. He apologizes and offers you an invitation, a dinner for two at their restaurant. But you have an important meeting to go to and have no time to change your outfit. What do you do?	
Possible Consequences	Solutions
Share your answers with a partner. In pairs, create a dialogue.	

5.

You have invited your coworker to dinner. You both start chatting and seem to have a lot in common. You notice that your guest has not touched the food yet, and you feel embarrassed, not knowing what the reason might be. He then tells you that he is Muslim and his religion does not permit him to eat pork. Both the appetizers and the main course are made with pork, and you don't have anything else in the refrigerator to offer him. What do you do or say?	
Possible Consequences	Solutions
Share your answers with a partner. In pairs, create a dialogue.	

6.

You are looking for your seat on the plane. To your surprise, your seat is taken by a disabled elderly person. The plane is full, and the only available seat is next to a family with two small children who are restless and cry a lot. You are tired and want to sleep. You need to be well rested for your audition the next day. What do you do?	
Possible Consequences	Solutions
Share your answers with a partner. In pairs, create a dialogue.	

7.

The water is warm, and both you and your friend enjoy the summer swim. You get out of the water and look for the towels and the few belongings you left on a lawn chair fifteen minutes ago. You now realize that your personal belongings along with your travel documents and money are gone. What do you do?	
Possible consequences	Solutions
Share your answers with a partner. In pairs, create a dialogue.	

8.

You are visiting a foreign country. You have the address of the landmark you want to see, and you ask the hotel receptionist for directions. He gives you brief directions, but you get lost and cannot find your way back. You don't speak the language, and it's getting dark. What do you do?	
Possible Consequences	Solutions
Share your answers with a partner. In pairs, create a dialogue.	

9.

It is about eleven o'clock at night, and you are on your way home from a concert. Your friends offered to give you a ride, but you refused, saying that you live close and the city is safe. The city seems deserted. Not too many people are walking at this hour of the night. You hear steps behind you. You take a right to cross the street, and the person crosses the street, too. You know that you are being followed. What do you do?

Possible Consequences	Solutions

Share your answers with a partner. In pairs, create a dialogue.

10.

Your classmate keeps asking you out, but you have other plans and don't want to get involved in a relationship. He is very attractive and very persistent. You have already told him that you are not interested, but in vain. You have just found out that he is in the middle of a divorce and has two small children. What do you say or do?

Possible Consequences	Solutions

Share your answers with a partner. In pairs, create a dialogue.

11.

You've neglected your homework and missed several class sessions. When you return to class, you don't understand the grammar points taught and are very worried. Moreover, you are not prepared for the upcoming test and might fail the finals. What do you do?

Possible Consequences	Solutions

Share your answers with a partner. In pairs, create a dialogue.

12.

A friend of yours invited you to a baby shower, but you forgot all about it. You were supposed to buy the gift and flowers and split the cost with your friend. When she calls to let you know that she'll pick you up in thirty minutes, you panic. You are just about to leave the house with your sister to attend a rock concert you've been waiting a long time for. What do you do?

Possible Consequences	Solutions

Share your answers with a partner. In pairs, create a dialogue.

13.

The weather is beautiful, perfect for the picnic. Your entire family is sitting on the grass and enjoying the gourmet dishes brought from home. Suddenly, the group of youngsters that was sitting next to you starts packing and carelessly leaves a lot of trash behind. You are frustrated to see so much carelessness. Hungry squirrels approach the pile of leftovers. What do you do?

Possible Consequences	Solutions

Share your answers with a partner. In pairs, create a dialogue.

14.

You have just arrived in a new country. You are at the airport and look forward to meeting your homestay family. You keep waiting and waiting, but the family that was supposed to greet you is nowhere to be seen. It has been an hour and a half since you arrived. You are hungry and tired, and you experience mixed feelings. You don't speak English and don't have a dictionary on you. What do you do?

Possible Consequences	Solutions

Share your answers with a partner. In pairs, create a dialogue.

Speak English for Success: ESL Conversations, Topics, and Dialogues   Lucia Gorea, Ph.D.

15.

You are walking alone on an empty street. Suddenly, someone comes from behind, grabs your purse, and runs away, without being seen at all. You panic. You want to scream for help, but there are no people around. You want to make a phone call, but you have no cash on you. What do you do?	
Possible Consequences	Solutions
Share your answers with a partner. In pairs, create a dialogue.	

16.

You are at a party, and some of your friends drink more than usual. Close to midnight, one of them grabs his car keys and wants to drive home despite everyone's pleading to stay. He says that he will be just fine and will take the freeway to avoid being stopped by the police. What do you do?	
Possible Consequences	Solutions
Share your answers with a partner. In pairs, create a dialogue.	

17.

It is about ten o'clock at night, and you are watching television. A loud crash comes from outside. You look out the window and see a hit-and-run accident. A person is lying on the sidewalk not able to move. What do you do?	
Possible Consequences	Solutions
Share your answers with a partner. In pairs, create a dialogue.	

18.

You were not feeling well last night and had to go to the hospital. You called your next-door neighbor to watch your child while you were gone. When you return from the hospital, neither the child nor the neighbor are in the house. You search everywhere, but the house is empty. What do you do?	
Possible Consequences	Solutions
Share your answers with a partner. In pairs, create a dialogue.	

19.

You are in line waiting to make a deposit at the bank. You are talking on your cell phone with a friend. Suddenly, a masked man enters the bank, points a gun at the bank teller, and asks for money. What do you do?

Possible Consequences	Solutions

Share your answers with a partner. In pairs, create a dialogue.

20.

You are calling long-distance and want to keep the conversation short. The person on the other line, who is in fact your future business partner, seems to be in the middle of a funny story. Out of courtesy, you don't want to interrupt him, but you don't want to pay a large telephone bill, either. What do you say?

Possible Consequences	Solutions

Share your answers with a partner. In pairs, create a dialogue.

Where Should They Go?

Three groups of ESL students, who are studying English at a community college in the United States, are planning a two-week summer vacation abroad. Before returning to their home countries, they want to spend some time together and have fun.

Student # 1. Your name is Mikhail.
        You are 23 years old.
        You are from Ukraine.
        Your hobbies are surfing and snorkeling.

You have never been to Italy, your dream vacation, and believe that this is the time when you can finally make your dream come true.
Try to convince your friends to choose Italy as a vacation destination.

Student # 2. Your name is Juanita.
        You are 21 years old.
        You are from Mexico.
        Your hobbies are singing and playing the piano.

You have never been to Japan, your dream vacation, and believe that this is the time when you can finally make your dream come true.
Try to convince your friends to choose Japan as a vacation destination.

Student # 3. Your name is Mohammed.
        You are 25 years old.
        You are from Saudi Arabia.
        Your hobbies are playing computer games and painting.

You have never been to Spain, your dream vacation, and believe that this is the time when you can finally make your dream come true.
Try to convince your friends to choose Spain as a vacation destination.

Student # 4. Your name is Martha.
        You are 22 years old.
        You are from Czechoslovakia.
        Your hobbies are writing poetry and surfing the internet.

After you have listened to your friends carefully, you will decide where your group of friends is going to spend the two-week vacation.

Student # 1. Your name is Kim.
        You are 19 years old.
        You are from China.
        Your hobbies are watching movies and reading science fiction.

You have never been to France, your dream vacation, and believe that this is the time when you can finally make your dream come true.
Try to convince your friends to choose France as a vacation destination.

Student # 2. Your name is Rose.
        You are 24 years old.
        You are from Kenya.
        Your hobbies are weaving and sewing.

You have never been to Canada, your dream vacation, and believe that this is the time when you can finally make your dream come true.
Try to convince your friends to choose Canada as a vacation destination.

Student # 3. Your name is Ralph.
        You are 20 years old.
        You are from Germany.
        Your hobbies are playing basketball and hiking.

You have never been to Africa, your dream vacation, and believe that this is the time when you can finally make your dream come true.
Try to convince your friends to choose Africa as a vacation destination.

Student # 4. Your name is Carlos.
        You are 21 years old.
        You are from Brazil.
        Your hobbies are playing soccer and music.

After you have listened to your friends carefully, you will decide where your group of friends is going to spend the two-week vacation.

Student # 1. Your name is Yoko.

You are 18 years old.

You are from Japan.

Your hobbies are gardening and shopping.

You have never been to Alaska, your dream vacation, and believe that this is the time when you can finally make your dream come true.

Try to convince your friends to choose Alaska as a vacation destination.

Student # 2. Your name is Alex.

You are 23 years old.

You are from Romania.

Your hobbies are playing the guitar and drawing.

You have never been to Australia, your dream vacation, and believe that this is the time when you can finally make your dream come true.

Try to convince your friends to choose Australia as a vacation destination.

Student # 3. Your name is Thien.

You are 24 years old.

You are from Vietnam.

Your hobbies are photography and knitting.

You have never been to Holland, your dream vacation, and believe that this is the time when you can finally make your dream come true.

Try to convince your friends to choose Holland as a vacation destination.

Student # 4. Your name is Razin.

You are 20 years old.

You are from Iran.

Your hobbies are swimming and playing chess.

After you have listened to your friends carefully, you will decide where your group of friends is going to spend the two-week vacation.

Finish the Dialogue

At the Restaurant

Frank: Good evening. I would like a table for two.
Waiter: Follow me, please.
Frank: Thank you.
Waiter: May I take your order?
Frank: Yes, what's on the menu?
Waiter: Our special today is _____
Frank _____
Waiter: _____
Frank: _____
Waiter: _____
Frank: _____
Waiter: _____

Your turn: In pairs, create a similar dialogue.

On the Street

Larry: Hi, John. It's nice to see you again.
John: Nice to see you, too, Larry.
Larry: I saw you yesterday with a beautiful woman.
John: Oh, yes, we were walking down Broadway Street.
Larry: Is she your wife?
John: Oh, no, she's _____
Larry: _____
John: _____
Larry: _____
John: _____
Larry: _____
John: _____

Your turn: In pairs, create a similar dialogue.

At the Travel Agency

Sharon: Hello. I plan to go on vacation next summer.
Agent: That's a great idea. What do you have in mind?
Sharon: I would like to go to Europe.
Agent: Europe? I can offer you great deals somewhere else.
Sharon: Well, I have never been to Italy, and…
Agent: Before you decide, let me show you what you can get for a better price to Mexico or Las Vegas.
Sharon: _____
Agent: _____
Sharon: _____
Agent: _____
Sharon: _____
Agent: _____

Your turn: In pairs, create a similar dialogue.

At Work

Julie: Susan, do you think I can ask Mrs. Black for a raise?
Susan: Yes, why not? How long have you been with the company?
Julie: Oh, it's been more than a year.
Susan: Then you can go ahead and ask her. She seems really nice.
Julie: I am a bit scared. Susan, how much do you make?
Susan: Oh, well, I'm afraid…
Julie: _____
Susan: _____
Julie: _____
Susan: _____
Julie: _____
Susan: _____

Your turn: In pairs, create a similar dialogue.

At a Party

Mary: I am not very fond of this party.
Jenny: Me neither. The food is not very good.
Mary: And the music is old-fashioned.
Jenny: The people aren't very friendly.
Mary: I'm bored. Let's go somewhere else.
Jenny: Good idea. Let's go…
Mary: _____
Jenny: _____
Mary: _____
Jenny: _____
Mary: _____
Jenny: _____

Your turn: In pairs, create a similar dialogue.

In Town

Sylvia: What do you feel like doing today? It's a rainy day.
Kenny: I don't know.
Sylvia: Would you rather go to the Portland Art Museum or to a concert?
Kenny: I think that we should stay home and play chess or do a jigsaw puzzle.
Sylvia: Are you sure you don't want to see some beautiful exhibits or listen to some classical music?
Kenny: Hmm…
Sylvia: _____
Kenny: _____
Sylvia: _____
Kenny: _____
Sylvia: _____
Kenny: _____

Your turn: In pairs, create a similar dialogue.

At the Library

Lucy: Brenda! What a surprise!
Brenda: Oh, Lucy, what are you doing here?
Lucy: I have to do a report for my English class. How about you?
Brenda: I'm doing research for my science class.
Lucy: Did you hear about Mark?
Brenda: No, what happened?
Lucy: _____
Brenda: _____
Lucy: _____
Brenda: _____
Lucy: _____
Brenda: _____

Your turn: In pairs, create a similar dialogue.

At the Hotel

Hotel Clerk: Hello, how can I help you?
Glen Baker: Hi. I booked a single room with a terrace and ocean view. I'm Mr. Glen Baker.
Hotel Clerk: Oh, yes. Your room number is 128 on the first floor. The rooms with ocean view and terrace are all taken. The only one available faces the parking lot.
Glen Baker: That's impossible. I made a reservation one month ago, and I have a confirmation number.
Hotel Clerk: I'm sorry. I don't think I can help…
Glen Baker: Who's the manager?
Hotel Clerk: _____
Glen Baker: _____
Hotel Clerk: _____
Glen Baker: _____
Hotel Clerk: _____
Glen Baker: _____

Your turn: In pairs, create a similar dialogue.

At the Department Store

Cashier: So, you have two shirts, a pair of shoes, a tie, a sports coat, and a pair of trousers.
Michael: Yes. And I'd like two bottles of soda, please.
Cashier: Cash or credit?
Michael: Credit, please.
Cashier: I'm sorry sir, but your credit card has been declined.
Michael: That's impossible!
Cashier: _____
Michael: _____
Cashier: _____
Michael: _____
Cashier: _____
Michael: _____

Your turn: In pairs, create a similar dialogue with the same title.

A Place to Rent

Leslie: Hi. Do you have a list of rentals for students?
Manager: Yes, we do. Are you looking for a room in a house or an apartment?
Leslie: A room in an apartment would be fine.
Manager: What exactly are you looking for?
Leslie: A neat and quiet place with nice, non-smoking roommates.
Manager: Let me see… Hmm… It seems like…
Leslie: _____
Manager: _____
Leslie: _____
Manager: _____
Leslie: _____
Manager: _____

Your turn: In pairs, create a similar dialogue with the same title.

Speak English for Success: ESL Conversations, Topics, and Dialogues

Lucia Gorea, Ph.D.

Find Someone Who

Write the name of a student who says *yes* to these questions.
Underline the phrasal verbs in the following sentences.

Find someone who	Name of Student
blew up when he saw that his car was towed away.	
cut back on coffee and unhealthy food.	
feels up to talking about an uncomfortable moment.	
looks like his or her mother.	
eats out three times a week.	
just got back from a trip to South America.	
gave up smoking and started a healthier life.	
likes to sing and is going to try out for the church choir.	
puts on makeup every day before leaving the house.	
gets along very well with all family members.	
dozed off while doing his or her homework.	
never let his teacher and classmates down.	
gets up at 7:30 a.m. every morning.	
has run out of gas and couldn't make it to work on time.	
always shows up late for class.	
got rid of some old clothes and bought new ones.	

Find Someone Who Would Like to

Write the name of a student who says *yes* to these questions. Write short answers to the questions below.

Find someone who would like to	Name of Student
travel around the world. (What places?) ---	
learn a new language. (What? Why?) ---	
buy a house. (Where? How big?) ---	
learn how to fly a plane. (Why?) ---	
apply for a job. (What?) ---	
learn how to play a musical instrument. (What? Why?) ---	
meet a famous political figure. (Whom? Why?) ---	
go bungee jumping. (When? Where?) ---	
write a biography. (Whose? When?) ---	
be on a TV show. (Which? Why?) ---	
learn a new dance. (What? Why?) ---	

Phrasal Verbs

Match each of the following phrasal verbs with their correct definition.

Phrasal Verbs	Meanings
___ 1. cross out	a. continue at the same rate
___ 2. do over	b. postpone
___ 3. fill out	c. leave unexpectedly, escape
___ 4. give up	d. submit
___ 5. hand in	e. to write information in blanks
___ 6. keep up	f. start to fly
___ 7. leave out	g. exercise
___ 8. let down	h. represent, permit
___ 9. make up	i. do again
___ 10. put off	j. put in the trash, discard
___ 11. run away	k. omit
___ 12. stand for	l. draw a line through
___ 13. show off	m. fail to support or help, disappoint
___ 14. take off	n. forgive each other
___ 15. throw away	o. act extra special for people watching(usually boastfully)
___ 16. work out	p. quit a habit

Answers: 1-l, 2-i, 3-e, 4-p, 5-d, 6-a, 7-k, 8-m, 9-n, 10-b, 11-c, 12-h, 13-o, 14-f, 15-j, 16-g.

Who's Talking?

Students take turns talking for two minutes about each topic.

Describe two family members.

_____

Describe your apartment or house.

_____

Talk about a funny situation.

_____

Talk about your favorite winter game.

_____

Explain how you prepare for an exam.

_____

Describe your math teacher.

_____

Describe the street you live on.

_____

Describe your best friend.

_____

Talk about a day in high school.

_____

Describe a trip to the zoo.

_____

Talk about an interesting experience you had when you were in a restaurant.

_____

Describe what would be your perfect place to live.

_____

Describe a busy market.

_____

Describe a day at home.

_____

Talk about your favorite fairytale.

_____

Describe the shopping mall in your neighborhood.

_____

Mix and Match (Set 1)

Print out a set of cards. Give each pair a set of shuffled cards, and have them match the phrasal verb with its definition. Students must use the phrasal verbs correctly in sentences of their own.

ask out	ask (someone) to go on a date
bring up	raise (children)
call off	cancel
drop in	visit without calling first
figure out	find the solution to a problem
find out	discover information
get along (with)	have a good relationship with
hang around (with)	spend undirected time

Mix and Match (Set 2)

Print out a set of cards. Give each pair a set of shuffled cards, and have them match the phrasal verb with its definition. Students must use the phrasal verbs correctly in sentences of their own.

keep on	continue
lay off	**stop employment**
look into	**investigate**
pick up	**lift**
put out	**extinguish a fire or a cigarette**
run into	meet by chance
show up	**come, appear**
tear down	**destroy a building**

Speak English for Success: ESL Conversations, Topics, and Dialogues

Lucia Gorea, Ph.D.

Role Playing

Put students in pairs, and give each pair several cards from the cut-up worksheet. The pairs read their situation and plan a role play.

Make a doctor's appointment.	Call to report a stolen car.
Make a reservation for a wedding reception at an expensive restaurant.	Ask for directions to the library.
Convince your classmate to read the book you have chosen for the English essay.	Explain to your parents why you failed the science exam.
Talk to a travel agent and reserve a round-trip flight.	Invite your coworkers to a housewarming party.
Call to report a hit-and-run accident.	Convince your friend to join you on a cruise to Alaska.
Explain to your partner how a healthy diet and exercise will help him or her lose the extra 20 pounds.	Ask your neighbor to baby-sit your two-month-old daughter.
Convince your boss that you need a raise.	Make an appointment to a beauty spa.

Correct the Sentences

Each of the following sentences contains mistakes. Can you find the mistakes and correct them?

1) I've seen him two day ago walking down Pine Street.

2) If I was twenty years old again, I choose a different profession.

3) Quiet! I trying to focus on this math problems.

4) I lived in this city since many years.

5) Peoples have to drink eight glass of water every day.

6) My MP3 isn't work. I has to fix it.

7) On his way home from work, Mary stopped at the grocery store to buy some coffees.

8) That chair is more comfortable then this one. Please seat down.

9) How long have Sam been leaving here?

10) Who's papers are this? Do you remember?

11) Their is a lot of informations in that encyclopedia.

12) I will have a Cobb salad for lunch. It taste more better than the Greek one.

13) Did you took English lessons before you arrives in the United States?

14) I flyed from Tokyo in Seattle first class.

15) Sarah has straight hairs, dark eyes, and weares glasses.

16) Its late. The movie have started half an hour ago.

17) Gina is more smarter than Jill. She study more hours every day.

18) Listen to me careful. If a stranger offer you a ride, always say no.

Find Someone Who

has the largest family	has the shortest hair
is slimmer than you	has bigger feet than you
is the tallest	speaks louder than you
has the most expensive car	is the youngest
has the best English accent	tells the best jokes
is more patient than you	is busier than you
has the best personality	cooks the spiciest meals

Find Someone Who

Write the name of a student who says *yes* to these questions.

1. _____ has passed an exam without studying at all.

2. _____ believes in life after death.

3. _____ treats his pets, dogs, or cats as members of his family.

4. _____ plans to attend college outside of his home country.

5. _____ knows how to design clothes.

6. _____ has played soccer in a league.

7. _____ attended a lecture on global warming.

8. _____ would like to donate to a charity.

9. _____ can recite a poem by heart.

10. _____ can name three classical pieces.

11. _____ can give two tips on how to study for the driver's license.

12. _____ has worked in dangerous jobs, such as the police or military.

13. _____ is going on a trip to South America.

14. _____ can speak four languages.

15. _____ knows what *ambidextrous* means.

16. _____ will compete in a marathon.

17. _____ remembers his first date.

18. _____ has never been sick.

Speak English for Success: ESL Conversations, Topics, and Dialogues   Lucia Gorea, Ph.D.

Mix and Match (Conditionals: Set 1)

Print out a set of cards. Divide the class into pairs. Distribute seven *If clause* sentences, and have students find their matches. Use the correct form of the verbs in parentheses.

If they were richer	you (catch) the last song.
If my friends (come, not) to my party	she wouldn't have failed the test.
If you had come earlier	I (make, not) so much noise.
If I weren't so hungry	they (buy) a bigger house.
If she (study) harder	I will look out the window before I open it.
If I had realized the baby was sleeping	I would have been very disappointed.
If someone (knock) on my door at night	I (share) my salad with you.

Speak English for Success: ESL Conversations, Topics, and Dialogues

Lucia Gorea, Ph.D.

Mix and Match (Conditionals: Set 2)

Print out a set of cards. Divide the class into pairs. Distribute seven *If clause* sentences, and have students find their matches. Use the correct form of the verbs in parentheses.

If the weather were nice today	we would have gone camping.
If James (quit, not) his job	this world would be a better place to live.
If I have enough cherries	I wouldn't have told anybody.
If people (hate, not) each other	we (take) a walk in the park.
If you exceed the speed limit while driving	he would have been promoted soon.
If Jay (asked) me to keep the news a secret	I (bake) a pie this afternoon.
If it (rain, not) so much	you (be) fined.

Tell Me Something

STUDENT A: Tell me something you have to do tomorrow.

STUDENT B: _____

STUDENT A: Tell me something that you should do to avoid accidents.

STUDENT B: _____

STUDENT A: Tell me something a good pilot should always do.

STUDENT B: _____

STUDENT A: Tell me something that parents must teach their children.

STUDENT B: _____

STUDENT A: Tell me something the government should do about discrimination.

STUDENT B: _____

STUDENT A: Tell me something you had to do last week.

STUDENT B: _____

STUDENT A: Tell me something a student must do to improve his or her English.

STUDENT B: _____

STUDENT A: Tell me something a person shouldn't do at a concert.

STUDENT B: _____

STUDENT A: Tell me something a teenager mustn't do at school.

STUDENT B: _____

STUDENT A: Tell me something a security guard should do at work.

STUDENT B: _____

STUDENT A: Tell me something a babysitter mustn't do.

STUDENT B: _____

STUDENT A: Tell me something you have to do to prepare for an earthquake.

STUDENT B: _____

STUDENT A: Tell me something a doctor mustn't do.

STUDENT B: _____

STUDENT A: Tell me something your friends shouldn't do.

STUDENT B: _____

Questionnaire

Write the missing words at the beginning of each sentence. Interview your partner, and write complete sentences on the lines provided below.

Where? Who? Whom? What kind of? Which? When? How often? What?

1. _____ meat do you eat most often?

   _____

2. _____ did you chat with after the exam?

   _____

3. _____ did you spend your honeymoon?

   _____

4. _____ did you graduate from high school?

   _____

5. _____ is your best friend?

   _____

6. _____ do you play chess?

   _____

7. _____ movies do you like best?

   _____

8. _____ would you like to talk to about your concerns?

   _____

9. _____ earrings are you going to buy?

   _____

10. _____ do you plan to celebrate New Year's Day?

    _____

11. _____ is your favorite poet?

    _____

12. _____ courses would you like to take next semester?

    _____

13. _____ was the last time you went to a concert?

    _____

14. _____ car would you like to drive?

    _____

Board Game: Roll the Dice (General Questions)

When you land on a star, ask a question.

START	★	Tell me what's in your purse. ⇨	How many pairs of shoes do you have?	LOSE A TURN	Talk about a situation when you were very disappointed. ⇩
How do you prepare your favorite food? ⇩	STAND UP AND STRETCH	What did your parents tell you not to do when you were a child?	Have you ever been to a tarot reader?	★	Name 5 countries in Europe. ⇦
What is the past tense form of the verb "keep"? ⇨	★	What is the scariest movie you have ever seen?	GO BACK 3 SPACES	Say the English alphabet in less than 8 seconds.	How many uncles and aunts do you have? ⇩
Name 5 things you will buy this week. ⇩	How do you celebrate the national holiday in your country?	Should teenagers date before the age of 15? Explain.	★	What can you find on a farm?	ROLL AGAIN ⇦
★	How many foreign countries have you visited? ⇨	Do you know someone who likes to gamble?	What is something you have never done in your life?	GO AHEAD 4 SPACES	What can you buy for $10,000? ⇩
What are your career goals? ⇩	What can a geologist do?	GO AHEAD 2 SPACES	What are your superstitions, if you have any?	Have you ever swum in a lake? ⇦	★
SING A SONG ⇨	What did your grandfather teach you?	★	ROLL AGAIN	What are your favorite winter sports?	☺ ☺ ☺ YOU WIN!

Board Game: Roll the Dice (General Questions)

When you land on a star, ask a question.

START	What does "kettle" mean?	GO AHEAD 2 SPACES	What will the world look like 100 years from now?	★	Name 5 vegetables. ⇩
Have you ever cheated on a test? If, so which one? ⇩	ROLL AGAIN	★	Is New York bigger or smaller than Paris? Describe 1 of the 2 cities.	What can you find at the beach?	Do you believe in ghosts? ⇦
★	What are the qualities of a friend? ⇨	Count from 124 to 196.	LOSE A TURN	Do you like taking naps? How often?	How do you usually spend your weekends? ⇩
How do you treat a sore throat? ⇩	ROLL AGAIN	Describe the best place you have ever been to.	Have you ever experienced an earthquake?	What do you pack when you go camping? ⇦	★
What are you going to do tomorrow night? ⇨	Describe some customs in your country.	What's in your refrigerator?	★	LOSE A TURN	Are you engaged? ⇩
What are you currently reading? ⇩	★	GO BACK 4 SPACES	Where do your relatives live?	Name the planets of our Solar System.	What is your philosophy about life after death? ⇦
Do you have a driver's license? ⇨	GO AHEAD 1 SPACE	When do people smile?	ROLL AGAIN	What is the antonym of "strength"?	☺ ☺ ☺ YOU WIN!

Speak English for Success: ESL Conversations, Topics, and Dialogues

Lucia Gorea, Ph.D.

Board Game: Roll the Dice (General Questions)

When you land on a star, ask a question.

START	How do you handle a complaint from your boss at work?	LOSE A TURN	What can you do to relax in a dentist's office?	★	Make 3 wishes. ⇩
What are the duties of a secretary? ⇩	Are home remedies effective in curing different ailments?	★	Draw a picture of how you will look 40 years from now.	Name 2 famous waterfalls.	ROLL AGAIN ⇦
GO AHEAD 1 SPACE ⇨	★	Which vegetables do you eat raw?	Recommend a book you have read recently. Explain.	Give some tips on how to control anger.	List 5 adverbs. ⇩
Describe the best party you have ever been to. ⇩	What is the lifestyle of a movie star?	What do people recycle?	★	SHAKE HANDS WITH 2 CLASSMATES	Describe what's in your living room. ⇦
ROLL AGAIN ⇨	Give a synonym of "obtain."	What toys did you play with when you were a child?	How can you protect your home from burglars?	★	What can you learn from being a volunteer? ⇩
★	Describe your dream house.	Give the forms of 3 irregular adjectives.	GO BACK 3 SPACES	What is a synonym of "persuade"?	What does "feast" mean? ⇦
What museums have you visited so far? ⇨	★	Talk about a historical event in your country.	LOSE A TURN	What does a cartographer do?	☺ ☺ ☺ YOU WIN!

Board Game: Roll the Dice (Vocabulary)

Use the following words in complete sentences, and give a short definition in your own words. When you land on a star, ask a question.

START	opportunity	★	thrilled	GO AHEAD 3 SPACES	researcher ⇩
threat ⇩	predictable	ROLL AGAIN	nocturnal	★	tribe ⇦
mystery ⇨	★	fuss	gaze	outsmart	LOSE A TURN ⇩
GO BACK 4 SPACES ⇩	segregated	persuasive	★	triumph	ignite ⇦
★	weary ⇨	nomad	ROLL AGAIN	proficient	ridge ⇩
charcoal ⇩	LOSE A TURN	inflate	obnoxious	prankster ⇦	★
deprived ⇨	★	jug	alleviate	villain	☺ ☺ ☺ YOU WIN!

Board Game: Roll the Dice (Synonyms and Antonyms)

Synonyms are words that have the same or almost the same meaning; for example, *small* and *little* are synonyms. Antonyms are words that have opposite meanings; for example, *small* and *big* are antonyms.

Give the synonym or the antonym of the following words.

START	synonym of *toss*	LOSE A TURN	synonym of *giant*	antonym of *failure*	★
★	antonym of *awful*	antonym of *smooth*	GO AHEAD 2 SPACES	synonym of *happen*	synonym of *require* ⇐
antonym of *spend* ⇒	ROLL AGAIN	synonym of *insect*	★	antonym of *absent*	synonym of *choose* ⇓
antonym of *loud* ⇓	★	synonym of *attempt*	antonym of *weak*	DO 5 JUMPING JACKS	synonym of *depart* ⇐
synonym of *start* ⇒	STAND UP AND WHISTLE	antonym of *fortunate*	LOSE A TURN	antonym of *wealthy*	★
ROLL AGAIN ⇓	★	synonym of *moist*	antonym of *agree*	antonym of *reject*	synonym of *accurate* ⇐
LOSE A TURN ⇒	synonym of *courteous*	GO BACK 3 SPACES	antonym of *heavy*	★	☺ ☺ ☺ YOU WIN!

Board Game: Roll the Dice (Occupations)

What does (a or an) _____ do? Example: *What does a painter do?* When you land on a star, ask a question.

START	secretary	★	nurse	LOSE A TURN	pharmacist ⇩
accountant ⇩	carpenter	butcher	ROLL AGAIN	★	locksmith ⇦
★	GO AHEAD 2 SPACES ⇨	pilot	plumber	housekeeper	attorney ⇩
gardener ⇩	painter	bus driver	★	GO BACK 1 SPACE	cashier ⇦
ROLL AGAIN ⇨	salesperson	grocer	janitor	LOSE A TURN	★
hairstylist ⇩	★	GO AHEAD 3 SPACES	construction worker	actor or actress	architect ⇦
pediatrician ⇨	GO BACK 2 SPACES	seamstress	★	fire fighter	☺ ☺ ☺ YOU WIN!

Board Game: Roll the Dice (Irregular Nouns)

Give the singular or the plural form of the following nouns. Then use them in sentences of your own. When you land on a star, roll the dice twice and ask a question.

START	singular of *children*	★	LOSE A TURN	plural of *deer*	singular of *women* ⇩
plural of *sheep* ⇩	★	GO BACK 3 SPACES	plural of *mouse*	singular of *teeth*	plural of *goose* ⇦
plural of *foot* ⇨	singular of *nuclei*	plural of *ox*	singular of *species*	ROLL AGAIN	★
GO AHEAD 2 SPACES ⇩	plural of *fish*	★	singular of *cacti*	plural of *man*	singular of *phenomena* ⇦
★	plural of *louse* ⇨	singular of *series*	plural of *offspring*	singular of *crises*	LOSE A TURN ⇩
plural of *moose* ⇩	plural of *bacterium*	NAME 5 NOUNS	singular of *syllabi*	★	singular of *data* ⇦
plural of *curriculum* ⇨	★	singular of *vitae*	LOSE A TURN	plural of *alumnus*	☺ ☺ ☺ YOU WIN!

Board Game: Roll the Dice (Irregular Verbs)

Give the irregular forms of the following verbs. Then use them in sentences of your own. When you land on a star, ask your partner the three forms of 5 irregular verbs.

START	past tense *steal*	past tense and past participle *write*	★	simple form *heard*	ROLL AGAIN ⇩
past tense *catch* ⇩	★	GO AHEAD 3 SPACES	simple form *began*	past participle *sweep*	past tense *speak* ⇦
past tense *cost* ⇨	GO BACK 2 SPACES	past participle *buy*	simple form *flew*	LOSE A TURN	★
GO AHEAD 1 SPACE ⇩	simple form *grown*	★	past participle *meet*	past tense *see*	past tense and past participle *hide* ⇦
★	past participle *sing* ⇨	past tense *drive*	GO BACK 1 SPACE	simple form *bent*	past tense *sleep* ⇩
simple form *fought* ⇩	past tense and past participle *know*	LOSE A TURN	past tense *swim*	★	past participle *run* ⇦
ROLL AGAIN ⇨	simple form *threw*	★	past tense and past participle *pay*	past tense *feel*	☺ ☺ ☺ YOU WIN!

Speak English for Success: ESL Conversations, Topics, and Dialogues

Lucia Gorea, Ph.D.

Board Game: Roll the Dice (Adjectives)

Add -er or *more* to form the comparatives of the words below. Then add -est or *the most* to form the superlatives of the words below. Finally, make sentences with each of the new forms. When you land on a star, ask a question.

START	wise	★	busy	difficult	LOSE A TURN ⇩
GO AHEAD 3 SPACES ⇩	happy	comfortable	helpful	★	nervous ⇦
★	expensive ⇨	ROLL AGAIN	courageous	heavy	pretty ⇩
narrow ⇩	delicious	smooth	★	humid	GO BACK 2 SPACES ⇦
boring ⇨	★	ugly	LOSE A TURN	empty	rich ⇩
ROLL AGAIN ⇩	interesting	funny	cute	short ⇦	★
terrific ⇨	noisy	★	GO BACK 4 SPACES	shallow	☺ ☺ ☺ YOU WIN!

Speak English for Success: ESL Conversations, Topics, and Dialogues
Lucia Gorea, Ph.D.

BOARD GAME: Roll the Dice (Modals)

Answer the following questions. When you land on a star, ask a question.

START	Would you ever consider traveling around the world alone? Why? Why not?	★	What should you do to get the job of your dreams?	GO AHEAD 1 SPACE	What can be done to reduce traffic accidents on the roads? ⇩
Should parents get involved in their children's marriages? Why? Why not? ⇩	LOSE A TURN	What must you do to prevent a cold?	Whom will you invite to your next birthday party? Name at least 5 people. ⇦	What is something a person ought to do to keep his or her job?	★
★	What should an athlete do to win a marathon? ⇨	Do you think that teenagers should chat online with strangers?	GO BACK 3 SPACES	What would you do if someone invited you to a concert you did not want to go to?	Must the government do something about unemployment? ⇩
ROLL AGAIN ⇩	How must you prepare for a university exam?	What might you do when a police car stops you?	★	What is something you should never ask a priest?	Where would you like to spend your next vacation? ⇦
Should people benefit from free health care? ⇨	★	LOSE A TURN	What can you find in a nursery?	What is something that you wouldn't eat or drink?	What is something a teacher ought to teach students? ⇩
Could you learn a foreign language in one month? ⇩	How should you prepare for a wedding?	Could you survive alone on a deserted island for 2 weeks?	What can you do to improve your pronunciation?	ROLL AGAIN ⇦	★
Tell me something you ought not to do in a church. ⇨	GO AHEAD 2 SPACES	★	What can you do to protect wildlife?	How can you teach a child to value honesty?	☺ ☺ ☺ YOU WIN!

Answer Key

Board Game: Synonyms and Antonyms

toss—throw / giant—huge / failure—success / awful—fantastic / smooth—rough
happen—occur / require—need / spend—save / insect—bug / absent—present
choose—pick or select / loud—quiet / attempt—try / weak—strong / depart—leave
start—begin / fortunate—unfortunate / wealthy—poor / moist—damp or wet /
agree—disagree / reject—approve / accurate—exact or precise / courteous—polite /
heavy—light.

Board Game: Adjectives

wiser—the wisest / busier—the busiest / more difficult—the most difficult /
happier—the happiest / more comfortable—the most comfortable / more helpful—
the most helpful / more nervous—the most nervous / more expensive—the most
expensive/ more courageous—the most courageous / heavier—the heaviest /
prettier—the prettiest / narrower—the narrowest / more delicious—the most
delicious / smoother—the smoothest / more humid—the most humid / more
boring—the most boring / uglier—the ugliest / emptier—the emptiest / richer—the
richest / more interesting—the most interesting / funnier—the funniest / cuter—the
cutest / shorter—the shortest more terrific—the most terrific / noisier—the noisiest
/ more shallow—the most shallow.

Appendix

List of Irregular Nouns

SINGULAR	PLURAL
axis	axes
analysis	analyses
basis	bases
crisis	crises
diagnosis	diagnoses
oasis	oases
parenthesis	parentheses
synopsis	synopses
thesis	theses

SINGULAR	PLURAL
appendix	appendices
index	indices or indexes
matrix	matrices or matrixes

SINGULAR	PLURAL
alumnus	alumni
cactus	cacti
focus	foci or focuses
fungus	fungi or funguses
nucleus	nuclei
radius	radii
stimulus	stimuli
syllabus	syllabi

SINGULAR	PLURAL
child	children
man	men
ox	oxen
woman	women

SINGULAR	PLURAL
bison	bison
deer	deer
fish	fish
means	means
moose	moose
offspring	offspring
series	series
sheep	sheep
species	species

SINGULAR	PLURAL
bacterium	bacteria
corpus	corpora
criterion	criteria
curriculum	curricula
erratum	errata
datum	data
medium	media
memorandum	memoranda
phenomenon	phenomena

SINGULAR	PLURAL
foot	feet
goose	geese
tooth	teeth

SINGULAR	PLURAL
antenna	antennae or antennas
formula	formulae or formulas
nebula	nebulae
vertebra	vertebrae
vita	vitae

SINGULAR	PLURAL
louse	lice
mouse	mice

List of Irregular Verbs

SIMPLE FORM	SIMPLE PAST	PAST PARTICIPLE	SIMPLE FORM	SIMPLE PAST	PAST PARTICIPLE
awake	awoke	awoken	keep	kept	kept
be	was, were	been	know	knew	known
become	became	become	lay	laid	laid
begin	began	begun	lead	lead	lead
bite	bit	bitten	leave	left	left
blow	blew	blown	lend	lent	lent
break	broke	broken	let	let	let
bring	brought	brought	lie	lay	lain
build	built	built	lose	lost	lost
burst	burst	burst	make	made	made
buy	bought	bought	meet	met	met
catch	caught	caught	pay	paid	paid
choose	chose	chosen	put	put	put
come	came	come	quit	quit	quit
cost	cost	cost	read	read	read
cut	cut	cut	ride	rode	ridden
deal	dealt	dealt	ring	rang	rung
dig	dug	dug	rise	rose	risen
do	did	done	run	ran	run
draw	drew	drawn	say	said	said
drink	drank	drunk	see	saw	seen
drive	drove	driven	seek	sought	sought
eat	ate	eaten	sell	sold	sold
fall	fell	fallen	send	sent	sent
feed	fed	fed	shake	shook	shaken
feel	felt	felt	sing	sang	sung
fight	fought	fought	sit	sat	sat
find	found	found	sleep	slept	slept
fly	flew	flown	speak	spoke	spoken
forbid	forbade	forbidden	spend	spent	spent
forget	forgot	forgotten	stand	stood	stood
forgive	forgave	forgiven	steal	stole	stolen
freeze	froze	frozen	swim	swam	swum
get	got	got/gotten	take	took	taken
give	gave	given	teach	taught	taught
go	went	gone	tell	told	told
grow	grew	grown	think	thought	thought
hang	hung	hung	throw	threw	thrown
have	had	had	understand	understood	understood
hear	heard	heard	wake	woke/waked	woken/waked
hide	hid	hidden	wear	wore	worn
hold	held	held	win	won	won
hurt	hurt	hurt	write	wrote	written

About the Author

Lucia Gorea, Ph.D., is a widely published writer, an award-winning poet, and an experienced English and ESL teacher. With degrees in English, French, and TESL, and a Ph.D. in English and Education, Dr. Gorea has taught Academic English, English as a Second Language, English Literature, and Language and Culture courses in universities and colleges in Canada, the United States and Europe.

Lucia is the author of several articles and books, including *ESL Games and Classroom Activities*, *Welcome to America! A Practical Guide to Life Survival Skills*, and *Journey Through My Soul*, a collection of love and mystical poems. She has performed readings and has given lectures in Canada and the U.S., and has made many television appearances on Rompost TV, Channel M. Lucia is a certified translator with the Canadian Translators, Terminologists and Interpreters and the founder and host of "Poetry Around the World," a multicultural poetry group. Lucia's biographical profile is included in *Who's Who of American Women*, *Who's Who in American Education*, *International Who's Who of Professional and Business Women*, and *Marquis Who's Who* encyclopedias.

Lucia has two manuscripts in print and is currently working on her first novel. She lives with her family in Vancouver, Canada, and teaches English and Intercultural Communication courses at the University of British Columbia.

To order a copy of
Speak English for Success: ESL Conversations, Topics, and Dialogues
please contact

AuthorHouse
1663 Liberty Drive
Bloomington, IN 47403
Ph: (888)-519-5121

Online
Lucia Gorea, Ph.D.
E-mail: gorea@cstudies.ubc.ca
E-mail: luciagorea@yahoo.ca